To May —
    with grateful
thanks for all you
mean to —

Petie & Milton

My Heart Kneels Too

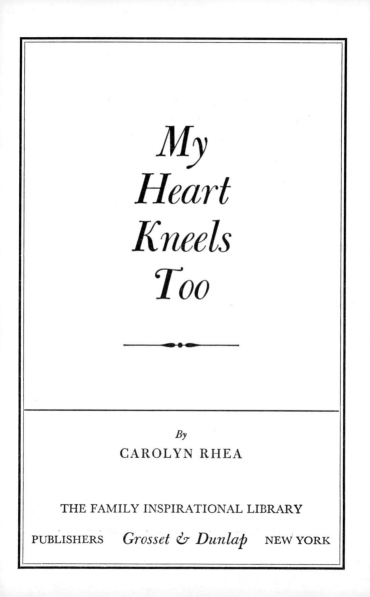

My Heart Kneels Too

By

CAROLYN RHEA

THE FAMILY INSPIRATIONAL LIBRARY

PUBLISHERS   *Grosset & Dunlap*   NEW YORK

PRINTED IN THE UNITED STATES OF AMERICA

From
My heart
to
CLAUDE'S

CONTENTS

I. LEARNING TO PRAY
My Heart Kneels Too 2
Believing 4
Distractions 6
Being Still 8
Catching Up 10
Voyage into Prayer 12
Reaching God Through Christ 14
Inoculation 16
In Jesus' Name 18
Prayer Choir 20
Gymnastics 22

II. FELLOWSHIP WITH GOD
Divine Restlessness 26
Photosynthesis of the Soul 28

In His Presence   30
Earthbound   32
Tracking Mud   34
Shared Dreams   36
Broken Fellowship   38
Trimming the Wick   40
Preface to Eternity   42

III. INTERCESSORY PRAYER
The Invisible Seesaw   46
Intensified   48
Telstar   50
Praying for my Children   52
Refreshing Fragrance   54

IV. LOOKING FOR THE ANSWER
Looking for the Answer   58
Distillation   60
When God Says "Yes"   62
When the Answer is "No"   64
When the Answer is "Wait"   66
Answered Prayer   68
Echoes   70

V. LEARNING THROUGH PRAYER
Awareness   74
Shadow Pictures   76
Mathematics   78
Merely Pity   80
Patchwork Quilt   82
Contact Lens   84

Pebbles of Prayer   86
Learning to Rejoice   88
The Puzzle   90
Potential   92
Practicing Prayer   94
Spiritual Delinquent   96
My Larger Family   98
Ski Lift   100

VI. WHEN WORDS DON'T COME
On Tiptoe   104
Abiding in Him   106
Tongue Tied   108
Volcanic Soil   110
The Spirit Intercedes   112

LEARNING TO PRAY

My Heart Kneels Too

I knelt to pray:

    Head bowed
      Eyes closed
        Hands folded
          Knees bent
But prayer did not come.

My proud and independent heart,
Defying man's humility and need,
Stood still unbowed in the presence of **God;**

And I could not pray
Until my heart knelt too.

MY HEART PONDERS . . .

If my people, which are called by my name, shall humble themselves, and pray, and seek my face, and turn from their wicked ways; then will I hear from heaven, and will forgive their sin, and will heal their land.   2 CHRONICLES 7:14

Let us lift up our heart with our hands unto God in the heavens.   LAMENTATIONS 3:41

Lord, my heart is not haughty, nor mine eyes lofty.
PSALM 131:1a

Every way of a man is right in his own eyes: but the Lord pondereth the hearts.   PROVERBS 21:2

Unite my heart to fear thy name.   PSALM 86:11b

Blessed are the pure in heart: for they shall see God.
MATTHEW 5:8

Believing

"Believing, ye shall receive!"

If only I could believe
And act upon it.

I find it easy to believe
That spring will follow winter,
That migratory birds won't lose their way,
That raging storms aren't everywhere at once,
That we continue to uncover healing for disease,
That an atom can be split,
That man will find his way through space.

Why should it be so hard
Simply to believe that God
Who gave me breath and life
Will answer when I pray?

MY HEART PONDERS . . .

But without faith it is impossible to please him: for he that cometh to God must believe that he is, and that he is a rewarder of them that diligently seek him. HEBREWS 11:6

And all things, whatsoever ye shall ask in prayer, believing, ye shall receive. MATTHEW 21:22

Jesus said unto him, If thou canst believe, all things are possible to him that believeth.

And straightway the father of the child cried out, and said with tears, Lord, I believe; help thou mine unbelief. MARK 9:23,24

What things soever ye desire, when ye pray, believe that ye receive them, and ye shall have them.
MARK 11:24b

But let him ask in faith, nothing wavering. For he that wavereth is like a wave of the sea driven with the wind and tossed. JAMES 1:6

Distractions

————

Why does my mind play leap-frog
When I try to pray,
Pouncing upon earthly thoughts and sounds
Quite foreign to my talk with God?

Why does it suddenly remember some forgotten
    deadline?
Or plan some future joy?
Or worry about something which might not
    even happen?

I bring my childish mind to Thee, O Lord,
With all its little whims.
Help it grow up, please.

MY HEART PONDERS . . .

When I was a child, I spake as a child, I understood as a child, I thought as a child: but when I became a man, I put away childish things. I Cor. 13:11

Casting down imaginations, and every high thing that exalteth itself against the knowledge of God, and bringing into captivity every thought to the obedience of Christ.   2 Cor. 10:5

Thou wilt keep him in perfect peace, whose mind is stayed on thee: because he trusteth in thee.
Isaiah 26:3

Let the words of my mouth, and the meditation of my heart, be acceptable in thy sight, O Lord, my strength, and my redeemer.   Psalm 19:14

Search me, O God, and know my heart: try me, and know my thoughts:
And see if there be any wicked way in me, and lead me in the way everlasting.   Psalm 139:23,24

Being Still

How difficult to be "still."

'Tis easier far to be busy than to be quiet,
To keep running harried, hectic missions
Or find some frail excuse to spin my rotors in
    the air and not come down;

But I must alight,
Turn off the rotors and be still,
So He who made this frail machine
Can check and clean and oil its parts,
Give instructions for my mission,
And pump in power to
Lift me up again.

MY HEART PONDERS . . .

Be still, and know that I am God: I will be exalted among the heathen, I will be exalted in the earth.
PSALM 46:10

He leadeth me beside the still waters.   PSALM 23:2b

But they that wait upon the Lord shall renew their strength; they shall mount up with wings as eagles; they shall run, and not be weary; and they shall walk, and not faint.   ISAIAH 40:31

And that ye study to be quiet.   1 THES. 4:11a

Then are they glad because they be quiet; so he bringeth them unto their desired haven.
PSALM 107:30

In quietness and in confidence shall be your strength.   ISAIAH 30:15b

Catching Up

I caught up with my praying
When thunder cracked the sky
And lightning sliced the world in half,
And twirling, pointed clouds looked like
Missiles waiting to be launched.

O yes, I prayed quite long and hard—
Enough to last until
    It storms again!

MY HEART PONDERS . . .

Pray without ceasing.   1 THES. 5:17

But we will give ourselves continually to prayer.
ACTS 6:4a

Praying always with all prayer and supplication in the Spirit.   EPHESIANS 6:18a

Peter therefore was kept in prison: but prayer was made without ceasing of the church unto God for him.   ACTS 12:5

But I give myself unto prayer.   PSALM 109:4b

He kneeled upon his knees three times a day, and prayed, and gave thanks before his God, as he did aforetime.   DANIEL 6:10b

Continue in prayer.   COL. 4:2a

Voyage Into Prayer

Prayer can be a canal whose locks lift me God-ward.

Upon entering the Canal of Prayer, I am lifted from the lowest level of praying merely for myself

Into the lock of true thanksgiving.

Upward I rise into the lock of intercession.

Higher still, I reach the peak of fellowship with God through praise and adoration.

Then gently I am lowered through the locks of self-surrender and dedication to His will and way

And discover that I exit on a higher plane!

Not every voyage into prayer is fully completed, for I am weak and immature

Yet its great potential will forever challenge me.

MY HEART PONDERS . . .

Give us this day our daily bread.

And forgive us our debts, as we forgive our debtors.
MATTHEW 6:11,12

Offer unto God thanksgiving.   PSALM 50:14a

Brethren, pray for us.   I THES. 5:25

I exhort therefore, that, first of all, supplications, prayers, intercessions, and giving of thanks, be made for all men.   1 TIM. 2:1

Sing forth the honour of his name: make his praise glorious.   PSALM 66:2

Our Father which art in heaven, Hallowed be thy name.
Thy kingdom come. Thy will be done in earth, as it is in heaven.
For thine is the kingdom, and the power, and the glory, forever.   Amen.   MATTHEW 6:9b,10,13b

Reaching God Through Christ

Where is God?
I need Him so!
How can I let Him know?

Is He visiting some distant star?
Untangling cosmic rays?
Creating vast new worlds?

Christ assured me that God cares
About my woe.

So I shall pray
And send that prayer to God
Through Christ.

MY HEART PONDERS . . .

For there is one God, and one mediator between
God and men, the man Christ Jesus;
Who gave himself a ransom for all.   1 Tim. 2:5,6a

No man cometh unto the Father, but by me.
John 14:6b

Seeing then that we have a great high priest, that
is passed into the heavens, Jesus the Son of God,
let us hold fast our profession.

For we have not an high priest which cannot be
touched with the feeling of our infirmities; but was
in all points tempted like as we are, yet without sin.

Let us therefore come boldly unto the throne of
grace, that we may obtain mercy, and find grace to
help in time of need.   Hebrews 4:14-16

Inoculation

I find myself in the long queue
Of those who pause in prayer
For quick inoculation against
Woes and ills and pain!
'Tis cheap protection
To be "immunized"
In such a simple way!

But I wonder. . . .
   Is that really
      What prayer is for?

MY HEART PONDERS . . .

What is it then? I will pray with the spirit, and I will pray with the understanding also. 1 Cor. 14:15a

And I say unto you, Ask, and it shall be given you; seek, and ye shall find; knock, and it shall be opened unto you.

For every one that asketh receiveth; and he that seeketh findeth; and to him that knocketh it shall be opened.

If a son shall ask bread of any of you that is a father, will he give him a stone? or if he ask a fish, will he for a fish give him a serpent?

Of if he shall ask an egg, will he offer him a scorpion?

If ye then, being evil, know how to give good gifts unto your children: how much more shall your heavenly Father give the Holy Spirit to them that ask him?   Luke 11:9-13

In Jesus' Name

"In Jesus' Name" is not the Abra-ca-da-bra to
   unlock a Genie God inside the lamp of
   prayer and bring Him to my beck and call.

Rather, it brings me to God in the right relationship in prayer;

For it affirms my faith in Christ,
   The Way—as Saviour
   The Truth—as Teacher
   The Life—as my Example

And reminds me that I must pray in harmony
   with this relationship.

It is this and even more.

MY HEART PONDERS . . .

Jesus saith unto him, I am the way, the truth, and the life: no man cometh unto the Father, but by me. John 14:6

And whatsoever ye shall ask in my name, that will I do, that the Father may be glorified in the Son. If ye shall ask any thing in my name, I will do it. John 14:13,14

At that day ye shall ask in my name: and I say not unto you, that I will pray the Father for you:

For the Father himself loveth you, because ye have loved me, and have believed that I came out from God. John 16:26,27

Whatsoever ye shall ask of the Father in my name, he may give it you. John 15:16b

The Prayer Choir

Together, as one,
We rose to pray—

God's great prayer choir!

In unison, our minds
Followed the one who led;
And our hearts harmonized—

Our "soul-melody" to God!

MY HEART PONDERS . . .

———

Let the people praise thee, O God; let all the people praise thee. PSALM 67:3

Making melody in your heart to the Lord.
EPHES. 5:19b

I will give thee thanks in the great congregation: I will praise thee among much people. PSALM 35:18

Singing with grace in your hearts to the Lord.
COL. 3:16b

That ye should shew forth the praises of him who hath called you out of darkness into his marvelous light. 1 PETER 2:9b

O magnify the Lord with me, and let us exalt his name together. PSALM 34:3

Gymnastics

I'm stretching muscles
I've seldom used before
In this daily exercise of prayer!

These early stages really are quite painful
while my

Heart muscles of love learn the lesson of reaching out to everyone

Leg muscles of faith carry me further than I've
dared to walk before

Mind muscles discern innumerable truths they've
never glimpsed before

Hand muscles stay busy serving every day.

MY HEART PONDERS . . .

———

Lord, teach us to pray. LUKE 11:1b

I give myself unto prayer. PSALM 109:4b

But as touching brotherly love ye need not that I write unto you: for ye yourselves are taught of God to love one another. 1 THES. 4:9

For we walk by faith, not by sight. 2 COR. 5:7

Open thou mine eyes, that I may behold wondrous things out of thy law. PSALM 119:18

Whatsoever thy hand findeth to do, do it with thy might. ECCLES. 9:10a

By love serve one another. GAL. 5:13b

FELLOWSHIP WITH GOD

Divine Restlessness

———

Water is driven by some strange yearning
To reach again the height
From whence it came.

My soul feels this yearning too;
For God created it to know discontent
With mere planes of Earth
And instilled this longing
To seek its rest in Him.

Through prayer, my restless soul
Reaches up to God.

MY HEART PONDERS . . .

As the hart panteth after the water brooks, so panteth my soul after thee, O God.

My soul thirsteth for God, for the living God.
PSALM 42:1,2a

Unto thee, O Lord, do I lift up my soul.
PSALM 25:1

My heart and my flesh crieth out for the living God. PSALM 84:2b

I will lift up mine eyes unto the hills, from whence cometh my help. PSALM 121:1

The Lord is good unto them that wait for him, to the soul that seeketh him. LAM. 3:25

Photosynthesis of the Soul

Prayer is photosynthesis of the soul.

The prayerless life is pale and wan
Grown solely in the shade of self,
But in that life exposed to God each day
In fellowship of prayer
Spiritual photosynthesis takes place.
The chlorophyll of faith
Responds to the light of His presence,
Producing vital sustenance for the soul.

MY HEART PONDERS . . .

For in him we live, and move, and have our being.
ACTS 17:28a

This then is the message which we have heard of him, and declare unto you, that God is light, and in him is no darkness at all.   1 JOHN 1:5

For he satisfieth the longing soul, and filleth the hungry soul with goodness.   PSALM 107:9

For the Lord God is a sun and shield.
PSALM 84:11a

In thy light shall we see light.   PSALM 36:9b

The Lord is my light and my salvation.
PSALM 27:1a

In His Presence

In His Presence my sins are quite apparent, and
I feel an urgency to rid myself of them.

In His Presence I feel His deep love through
Christ, and it warms my being.

In His Presence His Holy Spirit ministers to my
need—for strength, for comfort, for express-
ing how I feel.

In His Presence I sense His longing for all man-
kind to come to Him as Father too and see
that I must help to bring it about.

In His Presence I am inspired to seek higher
ground than I have trod before.

MY HEART PONDERS . . .

———

I said, Lord, be merciful unto me: heal my soul, for I have sinned against thee. PSALM 41:4

As the Father hath loved me, so have I loved you: continue ye in my love. JOHN 15:9

And I will pray the Father, and he shall give you another Comforter, that he may abide with you forever;
Even the Spirit of truth. JOHN 14:16,17a

And other sheep I have, which are not of this fold: them also I must bring, and they shall hear my voice; and there shall be one fold, and one shepherd. JOHN 10:16

And he said unto them, Go ye into all the world, and preach the gospel to every creature.
MARK 16:15

Be ye therefore perfect, even as your Father which is in heaven is perfect. MATTHEW 5:48

Earthbound

I'm Earthbound—
Cumbered with duties
And overweight with love for earthly things.
Why should I feel such discontent?
Why should my soul want wings?

According to earth's laws
The bumbling bumble bee
Really shouldn't fly at all,
And yet it does.

So in the miracle of prayer
My spirit soars to God.

MY HEART PONDERS . . .

And be not conformed to this world: but be ye transformed by the renewing of your mind, that ye may prove what is that good, and acceptable, and perfect, will of God. ROMANS 12:2

And I said, Oh that I had wings like a dove! for then would I fly away, and be at rest. PSALM 55:6

But they that wait upon the Lord shall renew their strength; they shall mount up with wings as eagles; they shall run, and not be weary; and they shall walk, and not faint. ISAIAH 40:31

Come unto me, all ye that labour and are heavy laden, and I will give you rest.

Take my yoke upon you, and learn of me; for I am meek and lowly in heart: and ye shall find rest unto your souls. MATTHEW 11:28,29

Tracking Mud

My little child comes rushing in to me,
Tracking mud upon the rug.
Shoes must be removed and cleaned,
And I must sweep the dirt away.

How like my little child am I!

Oftimes I've rushed into God's presence
Tracking Earth's dirt along with me.
Patiently and with loving kindness
He has scraped the mud of sin from me.

MY HEART PONDERS . . .

Wash me throughly from mine iniquity, and cleanse me from my sin.

For I acknowledge my transgressions: and my sin is ever before me.

Against thee, thee only, have I sinned, and done this evil in thy sight: that thou mightest be justified when thou speakest, and be clear when thou judgest.

Create in me a clean heart, O God; and renew a right spirit within me.

Restore unto me the joy of thy salvation; and uphold me with thy free spirit.   PSALM 51:2-4,10,12.

My little children, these things write I unto you, that ye sin not. And if any man sin, we have an advocate with the Father, Jesus Christ the righteous.
1 JOHN 2:1

Shared Dreams

The winter fury of the outside world
Doesn't seem so cold
When in prayer I sit around the fire with God.

Comfortable silence reigns.
No need for talk.
Just sit and dream of what I'd like to be and do,
Warm with the knowledge of having shared
    those dreams with God,

And when I face the icy blast outside,
I shall not be too cold.

MY HEART PONDERS . . .

And truly our fellowship is with the Father, and with his Son Jesus Christ.   1 JOHN 1:3b

To everything there is a season, and a time to every purpose under the heaven:
A time to keep silence, and a time to speak.
ECCLES. 3:1,7b

And that ye study to be quiet, and to do your own business, and to work with your own hands.
1 THES. 4:11a

Abide in me, and I in you. As the branch cannot bear fruit of itself, except it abide in the vine; no more can ye, except ye abide in me.

I am the vine, ye are the branches: He that abideth in me, and I in him, the same bringeth forth much fruit: for without me ye can do nothing.
JOHN 15:4, 5

Broken Fellowship

It's hard to pray, "I'm sorry."

Even though I practice well,
When I finally come to God
Somehow I cannot say it
And recite instead
Weak excuses in my defense.

God listens kindly to my chatter,
But there's a moat between;
And I feel miserably alone
Trying to save my injured pride.

But when at last with great relief I pray
"I'm truly sorry, God. Forgive me, please,
And help me make it right,"
The bridge of His forgiveness
Quickly falls across the moat
So I can walk again to Him.

MY HEART PONDERS . . .

But your iniquities have separated between you and your God, and your sins have hid his face from you, that he will not hear. ISAIAH 59:2

If we confess our sins, he is faithful and just to forgive us our sins, and to cleanse us from all unrighteousness. 1 JOHN 1:9

Have mercy upon me, O God, according to thy lovingkindness: according unto the multitude of thy tender mercies blot out my transgressions.
PSALM 51:1

For thou, Lord, art good, and ready to forgive; and plenteous in mercy unto all them that call upon thee. PSALM 86:5

Let the wicked forsake his way, and the unrighteous man his thoughts: and let him return unto the Lord, and he will have mercy upon him; and to our God, for he will abundantly pardon. ISAIAH 55:7

Trimming the Wick

All efforts to light the lamp of prayer
And ask God's forgiveness
    Were in vain.

The flame would flicker dimly and go out.

My neighbor's unforgiven hurts, still harbored
    in my heart,
Were encrusted on the wick
And had to be trimmed off completely
Before God's oil of lovingkindness could flow
    through freely
To feed the flame.

MY HEART PONDERS . . .

And forgive us our debts, as we forgive our debtors.
MATTHEW 6:12

Then the lord of that servant was moved with compassion, and loosed him, and forgave him the debt. But the same servant went out, and found one of his fellowservants, which owed him an hundred pence: and he laid hands on him, and took him by the throat, saying, Pay me that thou owest . . . Then his lord, after that he had called him, said unto him, O thou wicked servant, I forgave thee all that debt, because thou desiredst me: Shouldest not thou also have had compassion on thy fellowservant, even as I had pity on thee? . . . So likewise shall my heavenly Father do also unto you, if ye from your hearts forgive not every one his brother their trespasses. MATTHEW 18:27,28, 32,33,35

Preface To Eternity

Through prayer I'm learning something of
    Fellowship with God.

I seek Him out and learn of Him
As Master, Teacher, Father, Friend.

His greatness always towers above my little
    frame
Yet He in love bends down
Inspiring me to believe
That joy is mutual
When we're together.

Thus I sense His presence
Though through a glass darkly,
But these shared moments
Are preparing me for the eternal joy of His
    presence
Face to face someday.

MY HEART PONDERS . . .

Draw nigh to God, and he will draw nigh to you.
JAMES 4:8a

For now we see through a glass, darkly; but then face to face: now I know in part; but then shall I know even as also I am known. 1 COR. 13:12

Truly our fellowship is with the Father, and with his Son Jesus Christ. 1 JOHN 1:3b

He that dwelleth in the secret place of the most High shall abide under the shadow of the Almighty.
PSALM 91:1

Behold, what manner of love the Father hath bestowed upon us, that we should be called the sons of God.

Beloved, now are we the sons of God, and it doth not yet appear what we shall be: but we know that, when he shall appear, we shall be like him; for we shall see him as he is.   1 JOHN 3:1a,2

[43]

INTERCESSORY PRAYER

The Invisible Seesaw

I felt that someone prayed for me,
For there came an inner awareness
That someone cared enough to send through
    God
Remembrance of my heavy burden and my
    special need of Him.

It was as if God's mercy
Transformed that prayer into an
    invisible seesaw
Which lifted me while the weight of my burden
Rested briefly on the other end.

And with the lightened load, my tenseness
    thawed in the warm therapy of love and care
And new strength came now that I was more
    relaxed and trusting.

I knew that somewhere someone had prayed
    for me.

MY HEART PONDERS . . .

The grace of our Lord Jesus Christ be with you all.
2 THES. 3:18a

Now our Lord Jesus Christ, himself, and God, even our Father, which hath loved us, and hath given us everlasting consolation and good hope through grace,

Comfort your hearts, and stablish you in every good word and work. 2 THES. 2:16,17

For this cause we also, since the day we heard it, do not cease to pray for you, and to desire that ye might be filled with the knowledge of his will in all wisdom and spiritual understanding;

That ye might walk worthy of the Lord unto all pleasing, being fruitful in every good work, and increasing in the knowledge of God;

Strengthened with all might, according to his glorious power, unto all patience and long suffering with joyfulness. COL. 1:9-11

Now the Lord of peace himself give you peace always by all means. The Lord be with you all.
2 THES. 3:16

Intensified

Impartially, the sun shines alike on everyone.
(So does God's loving care!)
Yet those rays can be intensified
With a simple magnifying glass,
And that which is held beneath
Feels greater warmth.

So each day I place myself and others
'Neath God's magnifying glass of prayer
That we might feel in greater measure
His Love and Strength and Joy.

MY HEART PONDERS . . .

And this I pray, that your love may abound yet more and more in knowledge and in all judgment;

That ye may approve things that are excellent; that ye may be sincere and without offence till the day of Christ;

Being filled with the fruits of righteousness, which are by Jesus Christ, unto the glory and praise of God. PHIL. 1:9-11

Always in every prayer of mine for you all making request with joy. PHIL. 1:4

Now the God of peace, that brought again from the dead our Lord Jesus, that great shepherd of the sheep, through the blood of the everlasting covenant,

Make you perfect in every good work to do his will, working in you that which is wellpleasing in his sight, through Jesus Christ; to whom be glory for ever and ever.   Amen.   HEB. 13:20,21

Telstar

─────────

When I pray
For someone around the world,
Does he know?
Is it worth the worry spent?
Can it really help?

If human hands have fashioned
Telstar out in space
To bounce again to Earth
The words and image sent across the seas,

Surely God
Can re-direct my little prayer
Into that life
For whom I pray
And fuse with it
His wondrous love and care.

MY HEART PONDERS . . .

———

The effectual fervent prayer of a righteous man availeth much. JAMES 5:16b

Wherefore also we pray for always for you . . . That the name of our Lord Jesus Christ may be glorified in you, and ye in him, according to the grace of our God and the Lord Jesus Christ.
2 THES. 1:11a,12

Withal praying also for us, that God would open unto us a door of utterance, to speak the mystery of Christ, for which I am also in bonds:
That I may make it manifest, as I ought to speak.
COL. 4:3,4

Praying always with all prayer and supplication . . . And for me, that utterance may be given unto me, that I may open my mouth boldly, to make known the mystery of the gospel. EPHES. 6:18a,19

Finally, brethren, pray for us, that the word of the Lord may have free course, and be glorified, even as it is with you:

And that we may be delivered from unreasonable and wicked men: for all men have not faith.
2 THES. 3:1,2

Praying For My Children

When God placed these little bulbs in the
 garden of my care to tend these years
 before as bulbs again they return to
 Him once more,

I felt quite helpless in knowing how to
 nourish them so they would reach maturity;

And so each day in prayer I ask Him what
 to do . . . whether I should water, prune,
 or spray, or add something to enrich
 the soil.

(Sometimes they're almost wilted from a
 moment of neglect or when I fail to do
 as He directs.)

But oh, the joy we share as little buds appear
 from which the blooms will come!

MY HEART PONDERS . . .

Lo, children are an heritage of the Lord.

PSALM 127:3a

Thy children like olive plants round about thy table. PSALM 128:3b

Children, obey your parents in the Lord: for this is right.

And, ye fathers, provoke not your children to wrath: but bring them up in the nurture and admonition of the Lord.   EPHESIANS 6:1,4

But continue thou in the things which thou hast learned and hast been assured of, knowing of whom thou hast learned them;

And that from a child thou hast known the holy scriptures, which are able to make thee wise unto salvation through faith which is in Christ Jesus.

2 TIM. 3:14,15

[53]

Refreshing Fragrance

Someone prayed for me as I went about my
daily tasks,

And that prayer was wafted through the
air

As a refreshing fragrance

And brought a breath of Spring into my
life.

MY HEART PONDERS . . .

We give thanks to God always for you all, making mention of you in our prayers.   1 Thes. 1:2

Always in every prayer of mine for you all making request with joy. Phil. 1:4

I thank God, whom I serve from my forefathers with pure conscience, that without ceasing I have remembrance of thee in my prayers night and day.
2 Tim. 1:3

The Lord Jesus Christ be with thy spirit. Grace be with you. Amen. 2 Tim. 4:22

Peace be with you all that are in Christ Jesus. Amen. 1 Peter 5:14b

I thank my God, making mention of thee always in my prayers.   Philemon 4

LOOKING FOR THE ANSWER

Looking For The Answer

———

I made a request of God in prayer.
Now I'm looking for the answer.
I'm certain it will come,
But I never know just how.
Sometimes He lets me know directly
Or sends it by a friend
Or even has me follow step by step
His notches in the forest
As He leads the way ahead.

MY HEART PONDERS . . .

Ask, and it shall be given you; seek, and ye shall find; knock, and it shall be opened unto you:

For everyone that asketh receiveth; and he that seeketh findeth; and to him that knocketh it shall be opened. MATTHEW 7:7,8

For your Father knoweth what things ye have need of, before ye ask him. MATTHEW 6:8b

And it shall come to pass, that before they call, I will answer; and while they are yet speaking, I will hear. ISAIAH 65:24

Consider and hear me, O Lord my God: lighten mine eyes. PSALM 13:3a

Hear my prayer, O Lord, give ear to my supplications: in thy faithfulness answer me, and in thy righteousness. PSALM 143:1

Distillation

Take my prayer requests, O Lord,
So full of life's impurities
And distill them in Thy love.

Remove from them the earthiness
Which tinges everything I ask;
Then teach me how to gladly drink
The pure and living water
Thou sendest down to me.

MY HEART PONDERS . . .

And he went a little farther, and fell on his face, and prayed, saying, O my Father, if it be possible, let this cup pass from me: nevertheless not as I will, but as thou wilt. MATTHEW 26:39

Thy will be done in earth, as it is in heaven.
MATTHEW 6:10b

Teach me to do thy will; for thou art my God: thy spirit is good; lead me into the land of uprightness. PSALM 143:10

I delight to do thy will, O my God: yea, thy law is within my heart. PSALM 40:8

Thy will be done, as in heaven, so in earth.
LUKE 11:2b

When God Says "Yes"

I feel the ecstasy of a little child
    with some new toy every time God
    answers "Yes" to my request.

There is a tinge of wonder and of awe
    that it's really mine—that He saw
    fit to grant that which I asked;

But the test of my gratitude lies just
    ahead—whether I abuse the gift or
    use it so that it will honor God.

MY HEART PONDERS . . .

For this child I prayed; and the Lord hath given me my petition which I asked of him:

Therefore also I have lent him to the Lord; as long as he liveth he shall be lent to the Lord . . .

1 Sam. 1:27,28a

And Hannah prayed, and said, My heart rejoiceth in the Lord . . .   1 Sam. 2:1a

Peter therefore was kept in prison: but prayer was made without ceasing of the church unto God for him.

And, behold, the angel of the Lord came upon him, and a light shined in the prison: and he smote Peter on the side, and raised him up, saying, Arise up quickly. And his chains fell off from his hands. And he went out, and followed him . . .
. . . He came to the house of Mary the mother of John, whose surname was Mark; where many were gathered together praying.   Acts 12:5,7,9a,12b

When The Answer Is "No"

Oftimes as a parent I've refused my child's
    request, knowing it would bring harm to
    him or others if I granted it.

Why, then, should I feel so rebellious when
    God's answer is "no"

And fail to discern that it is really a
    valentine from His heart to mine

With the message tucked inside that His love
    could not grant that which would have
    crippled my potential and compromised my
    finest self.

MY HEART PONDERS . . .

Ye ask, and receive not, because ye ask amiss.
JAMES 4:3a

And lest I should be exalted above measure through the abundance of the revelations, there was given to me a thorn in the flesh, the messenger of Satan to buffet me, lest I should be exalted above measure.

For this thing I besought the Lord thrice, that it might depart from me.

And he said unto me, My grace is sufficient for thee: for my strength is made perfect in weakness. Most gladly therefore will I rather glory in my infirmities, that the power of Christ may rest upon me.   2 COR. 12:7-9

When The Answer Is "Wait"

I became impatient when God's answer to my
  prayer was "Wait";

But He helped me plant and harvest other
  crops as seasons came and passed, and each
  left rich deposits in the soil of my life.

God's time evolved at last, and the gift I
  asked for long ago was granted.

It flourished now in soil enriched and
  mellowed through the years.

Then I understood why God had answered,
  "Wait."

MY HEART PONDERS . . .

Rest in the Lord, and wait patiently for him.
PSALM 37:7a

Wait on the Lord: be of good courage, and he shall strengthen thine heart: wait, I say, on the Lord. PSALM 27:14

Truly my soul waiteth upon God. PSALM 62:1a

My soul, wait thou only upon God; for my expectation is from him. PSALM 62:5

But thou art the same, and thy years shall have no end. PSALM 102:27

I wait for the Lord, my soul doth wait, and in his word do I hope. PSALM 130:5

Answered Prayer

If you rise from prayer, forgiven and clean
inside, prayer has been answered.

If you rise, more conscious of His greatness,
His goodness, His mercy, His love, His
nearness, prayer has been answered.

If you rise with greater love and compassion for
your fellowman, answered prayer is
transforming your selfish nature.

If you rise with an abiding sense of peace even
in the midst of great problems or sorrow,
God has answered by helping you meet
them.

If you rise with clearer vision, greater purpose,
positive direction, renewed strength, fresh
inspiration, prayer has been answered.

MY HEART PONDERS . . .

And this is the confidence that we have in him, that, if we ask anything according to his will, he heareth us:

And if we know that he hear us, whatsoever we ask, we know that we have the petitions that we desired of him.   1 JOHN 5:14,15

But thanks be to God, which giveth us the victory through our Lord Jesus Christ. 1 COR. 15:57

We are troubled on every side, yet not distressed; we are perplexed, but not in dispair. 2 COR. 4:8

I called upon the Lord in distress: the Lord answered me, and set me in a large place. PSALM 118:5

When I fall, I shall arise; when I sit in darkness, the Lord shall be a light unto me. MICAH 7:8b

Echoes

If I humbly confess my sin and ask God's forgiveness, others will see how much cleaner my life is.

If I seek inspiration from God for daily living, it will ignite a visible spark in my life.

If I take my fears to Jesus, others can see that my fears do not possess me.

If I seek wisdom and understanding from God, others will read it in the pages of my life.

If I truly seek His will, others will know it by the paths I choose to take.

If I have true fellowship with God through prayer, others will sense His nearness too.

MY HEART PONDERS . . .

And they took knowledge of them, that they had been with Jesus.   Acts 4:13b

But the path of the just is as the shining light, that shineth more and more unto the perfect day.
                                                                Prov. 4:18

And maketh manifest the savour of his knowledge by us in every place.   2 Cor. 2:14b

But the wisdom that is from above is first pure, then peaceable, gentle, and easy to be entreated, full of mercy and good fruits, without partiality, and without hypocrisy.   James 3:17

Little children, let no man deceive you: he that doeth righteousness is righteous, even as he is righteous.   1 John 3:7

That ye may be blameless and harmless, the sons of God, without rebuke, in the midst of a crooked and perverse nation, among whom ye shine as lights in the world.   Phil. 2:15

LEARNING THROUGH PRAYER

Awareness

———————

In moments of prayer I recognize the presence
    of God

And comprehend that He is very near me all
    the time,

But busy living crowds that sense of nearness
    from my thoughts.

It seems as though I even try to shut myself
    off from Him

So I can freely go my selfish way;

But when I pause to open wide the door of
    prayer,

I see that He is there.

MY HEART PONDERS . . .

That they should seek the Lord, if haply they might feel after him, and find him, though he be not far from every one of us. ACTS 17:27

The eyes of the Lord are in every place, beholding the evil and the good. PROV. 15.3

Whither shall I go from thy spirit? or whither shall I flee from thy presence?
If I ascend up into heaven, thou art there: if I make my bed in hell, behold, thou art there.
If I take the wings of the morning, and dwell in the uttermost parts of the sea;
Even there shall thy hand lead me, and thy right hand shall hold me. PSALM 139:7-10

The eyes of the Lord are upon the righteous, and his ears are open unto their cry. PSALM 34:15

Shadow Pictures

———

I'm quite adept at casting poses of piosity
    for those around to see!

With dexterity of fingers and skillful lights

I create little shadow pictures to parade
    across the wall;

But God's light is full upon me when I pray

And unveils my little game.

MY HEART PONDERS . . .

And when thou prayest, thou shalt not be as the
hypocrites are: for they love to pray standing in
the synagogues and in the corners of the streets,
that they may be seen of men. Verily I say unto
you, They have their reward. MATT. 6:5

Two men went up into the temple to pray; the one
a Pharisee, and the other a publican.
The Pharisee stood and prayed thus with himself,
God, I thank thee, that I am not as other men are,
extortioners, unjust, adulterers, or even as this publican.
I fast twice in the week, I give tithes of all that I
possess.
And the publican, standing afar off, would not
lift up so much as his eyes unto heaven, but smote
upon his breast, saying, God be merciful to me a
sinner. LUKE 18:10-13

Mathematics

How exciting to discover the mathematics
    of prayer!

It adds to my faith (which hitherto was very
    small)

Substracts my fears (which are too numerous
    to count)

Multiplies my understanding (so I can
    cooperate with God)

Divides my sole loyalty to Earth (for I
    glimpse joys of Heaven in prayer's
    fellowship with God).

MY HEART PONDERS . . .

And the apostles said unto the Lord, Increase our faith. LUKE 17:5

So that we may boldly say, The Lord is my helper, and I will not fear what man shall do unto me.
HEBREWS 13:6

If any of you lack wisdom, let him ask of God, that giveth to all men liberally, and upbraideth not; and it shall be given him. JAMES 1:5

Eye hath not seen, nor ear heard, neither have entered into the heart of man, the things which God hath prepared for them that love him.

But God hath revealed them unto us by his Spirit: for the Spirit searcheth all things, yea, the deep things of God. 1 COR. 2:9b,10

Merely Pity

I stood and stared at such an abject human
    being.

Pity stung my heart, but soon the stinging
    eased and I moved on.

Then on my knees in prayer I learned the
    lesson of compassion—

That when I see someone in need,
I should stop to help, to pray, or seek for aid.

Pity is not enough
For Pity stands and stares.
Compassion sees and serves.

MY HEART PONDERS . . .

———

And Jesus answering said, A certain man went down from Jerusalem to Jericho, and fell among thieves, which stripped him of his raiment, and wounded him, and departed, leaving him half dead.

And by chance there came down a certain priest that way: and when he saw him, he passed by on the other side.

And likewise a Levite, when he was at the place, came and looked on him, and passed by on the other side.

But a certain Samaritan, as he journeyed, came where he was: and when he saw him, he had compassion on him,

And went to him, and bound up his wounds, pouring in oil and wine, and set him on his own beast, and brought him to an inn, and took care of him.

LUKE 10:30-34

Patchwork Quilt

———

The many, many blessings for which I thank
    God day by day are multi-colored patches
    in my quilt of prayer.

At times I'm prone to shiver, feeling urgent
    need for something more

But nestled 'neath my patchwork quilt of
    God's remembered blessings

I find I'm truly warm enough!

MY HEART PONDERS . . .

Bless the Lord, O my soul, and forget not all his benefits:
Who forgiveth all thine iniquities; who healeth all thy diseases;
Who redeemeth thy life from destruction; who crowneth thee with lovingkindness and tender mercies;
Who satisfieth thy mouth with good things.

PSALM 103:2-5a

Giving thanks unto the Father. COL. 1:12a

Every good gift and every perfect gift is from above, and cometh down from the Father of lights, with whom is no variableness, neither shadow of turning. JAMES 1:17

The Lord hath done great things for us; whereof we are glad. PSALM 126:3

Contact Lens

I didn't know I was near-sighted
'Til I discovered it in prayer.
I had thought that everyone
Saw only blurred images
Of those in the distance
Outside the circle of nearness;

But when I truly prayed
That God would show me how to serve,
It was as if He quietly slipped into my eyes
Contact lens.
For when I opened them,
Suddenly, in clear focus, I saw
Even those quite far from me—
The burdens some were bearing
The joylessness of others
Their deep need for Christ's redeeming love.

MY HEART PONDERS . . .

The eyes of your understanding being enlightened.

EPHES. 1:18a

Then Peter opened his mouth, and said, Of a truth
I perceive that God is no respecter of persons:

But in every nation he that feareth him, and
worketh righteousness, is accepted with him.

And he commanded us to preach unto the people,
and to testify that it is he which was ordained of
God to be the Judge of quick and dead.

ACTS 10:34,35,42

He that loveth his brother abideth in the light, and
there is none occasion of stumbling in him.

But he that hateth his brother is in darkness, and
walketh in darkness, and knoweth not whither he
goeth, because that darkness hath blinded his eyes.

1 JOHN 2:10,11

Pebbles of Prayer

As each Christian
Drops a pebble of prayer
Into God's great sea of Love,
The ever widening circles
That they make
Merge each into the other
In bonds of Christian
Fellowship and love.

MY HEART PONDERS . . .

That which we have seen and heard declare we unto you, that ye also may have fellowship with us: and truly our fellowship is with the Father, and with his Son Jesus Christ.

But if we walk in the light, as he is in the light, we have fellowship one with another.

1 John 1:3,7a

And the Lord make you to increase and abound in love one toward another, and toward all men, even as we do toward you. 1 Thes. 3:12

That their hearts might be comforted, being knit together in love. Col. 2:2a

He that loveth his brother abideth in the light, and there is none occasion of stumbling in him.

1 John 2:10

Learning to Rejoice

I felt it wasn't fair
For my neighbor to have both salt and pepper
    to flavor life when my own was
        quite tasteless!

I took my envy straight to God in prayer.

He called to my remembrance how quick I was
    to weep with her when sorrow came,

And then He taught the counter-part—

    To rejoice when there is joy.

MY HEART PONDERS . . .

Rejoice with them that do rejoice, and weep with them that weep. ROMANS 12:15

And let none of you imagine evil in your hearts against his neighbour. ZECH. 8:17a

Thou shalt love thy neighbour as thyself.
MARK 12:31b

Love worketh no ill to his neighbour: therefore love is the fulfilling of the law. ROMANS 13:10

An hypocrite with his mouth destroyeth his neighbour: but through knowledge shall the just be delivered. PROV. 11:9

See that none render evil for evil unto any man; but ever follow that which is good, both among yourselves, and to all men. 1 THES. 5:15

The Puzzle

My Heavenly Father is never too busy to
    listen to all the many "little" things
    I tell Him every day.

Tenderly He watches as I sort the peices
    of my puzzle

And as they interlock, I begin to see
    patterns of light and shade and then
    the whole design my day has made.

There before us lie my strengths and weaknesses,
    my progress and my fears, and I can see
    the larger needs for which I now must pray.

MY HEART PONDERS . . .

In everything by prayer and supplication with thanksgiving let your requests be made known unto God. PHIL. 4:6b

Let us therefore come boldly unto the throne of grace, that we may obtain mercy, and find grace to help in time of need. HEB. 4:16

Cause me to know the way wherein I should walk; for I lift up my soul unto thee. PSALM 143:8b

Search me, O God, and know my heart: try me, and know my thoughts:
And see if there be any wicked way in me, and lead me in the way everlasting. PSALM 139:23,24

If any of you lack wisdom, let him ask of God, that giveth to all men liberally, and upbraideth not; and it shall be given him. JAMES 1:5

Potential

If prayer, when taken
Merely as an aspirin
Swallowed with one quick gulp
Can help to ease my aches and pains,
What is its true potential?

I tremble to think that maybe God
Through prayer
Could unleash His healing rays
To help restore one
Broken in spirit or body.

MY HEART PONDERS . . .

Is any among you afflicted? let him pray.
Is any merry? let him sing psalms.

Is any sick among you? let him call for the elders
of the church; and let them pray over him, anoint-
ing him with oil in the name of the Lord:

And the prayer of faith shall save the sick, and the
Lord shall raise him up; and if he have committed
sins, they shall be forgiven him.

Confess your faults one to another, and pray for
one another, that ye may be healed. The effectual
fervent prayer of a righteous man availeth much.

JAMES 5:13-16

But unto you that fear my name shall the Sun of
righteousness arise with healing in his wings.

MALACHI 4:2a

Practicing Prayer

If only I would practice prayer
As diligently as piano!

Stiff fingers striking discord
Practice o'er and o'er again
Until the notes are smooth and right
As the composer wrote.

If I would daily practice
On the keyboard of prayer,
Surely I would master
Lovely melodies from God.

MY HEART PONDERS . . .

And it came to pass in those days, that he went out into a mountain to pray, and continued all night in prayer to God. LUKE 6:12

And in the morning, rising up a great while before day, he went out, and departed into a solitary place, and there prayed. MARK 1:35

But thou, when thou prayest, enter into thy closet, and when thou hast shut thy door, pray to thy Father which is in secret; and thy Father which seeth in secret shall reward thee openly. MATT. 6:6

And when he had sent the multitudes away, he went up into a mountain apart to pray: and when the evening was come, he was there alone.
MATT. 14:23

Continue in prayer, and watch in the same with thanksgiving. COL. 4:2

Spiritual Delinquent

This stubborn, adolescent will of mine
Is making me a spiritual delinquent!

It drives me recklessly about on life's
    freeways,
At times endangering both myself and
    others along the way.

If I bring it daily unto God in prayer,
Surely He can curb these tendencies
    With His understanding love
And gently bend it to His will and way
During this difficult period of growing up
Toward spiritual maturity.

MY HEART PONDERS . . .

For the good that I would I do not: but the evil which I would not, that I do.

Now if I do that I would not, it is no more I that do it, but sin that dwelleth in me. ROM. 7:19,20

Submit yourselves therefore to God. Resist the devil, and he will flee from you.

Draw nigh to God, and he will draw nigh to you. Cleanse your hands, ye sinners; and purify your hearts, ye double minded. JAMES 4:8

Enter ye in at the strait gate: for wide is the gate, and broad is the way, that leadeth to destruction, and many there be which go in thereat:

Because strait is the gate, and narrow is the way, which leadeth unto life, and few there be that find it. MATT. 7:13,14

My Larger Family

Even in repose at night
Instinctively I hear
Each childish footfall, cough, or sound
And rise to minister to
    My little family.

Prayer tunes my heart to others' needs
So I can hear their plea for comfort,
    strength, and aid,
And helps me gladly to arise
And minister to those who comprise
My Larger Family through Christ.

MY HEART PONDERS . . .

Then shall the King say . . .

For I was an hungred, and ye gave me meat: I was thirsty, and ye gave me drink: I was a stranger, and ye took me in:

Naked, and ye clothed me: I was sick, and ye visited me: I was in prison, and ye came unto me.

Then shall the righteous answer him, saying, Lord, when saw we thee an hungred, and fed thee? or thirsty, and gave thee drink?

When saw we thee a stranger, and took thee in?

And the King shall answer and say unto them, Verily I say unto you, Inasmuch as ye have done it unto one of the least of these my brethren, ye have done it unto me.   MATTHEW 25:34a,35,36,37, 38a,40

Ski Lift

———

Far below I gazed up at the summit
And dreamed of being there,
But these frail legs couldn't
Scale the height.

And then I found a way—
The ski lift of prayer!

Sitting still inside the chair,
I watched it draw me up the slopes.
Breathlessly I glimsed broad vistas
And viewed with new perspective the
    tiny path I'd trod
And breathed great gulps of God's
    refreshing air
And let my mind and heart and soul
Run free in God's expanse of time.

Then with a leap of faith
I skiied to earth again.

MY HEART PONDERS . . .

I will lift up mine eyes unto the hills, from whence cometh my help.

My help cometh from the Lord, which made heaven and earth.   PSALM 121:1,2

That the God of our Lord Jesus Christ, the Father of glory, may give unto you the spirit of wisdom and revelation in the knowledge of him:

The eyes of your understanding being enlightened; that ye may know what is the hope of his calling, and what the riches of the glory of his inheritance in the saints,

And what is the exceeding greatness of his power to usward who believe.   EPHESIANS 1:17-19a

May be able to comprehend with all saints what is the breadth, and length, and depth, and height;

And to know the love of Christ, which passeth knowledge, that ye might be filled with all the fulness of God.   EPHESIANS 3:18,19

WHEN WORDS DON'T COME

On Tiptoe

There are moments of breathless awe
    in which I'm overwhelmed with the
      majesty of God

And tremble with the thought that I,
    a creature of His hand, can fellowship
      with the Divine.

Somehow I cannot rush right in to prayer
but stand on tiptoe just outside.

MY HEART PONDERS...

———

When I consider thy heavens, the work of thy fingers, the moon and the stars, which thou hast ordained;

What is man, that thou art mindful of him? and the son of man, that thou visitest him?

PSALM 8:3,4

O Lord, how great are thy works! and thy thoughts are very deep.   PSALM 92:5

For my thoughts are not your thoughts, neither are your ways my ways, saith the Lord.

For as the heavens are higher than the earth, so are my ways higher than your ways, and my thoughts than your thoughts.   ISAIAH 55:8,9

O come, let us worship and bow down: let us kneel before the Lord our maker.   PSALM 95:6

Abiding In Him

How shall I pray for one so dear
Whose thread of life is so near breaking?

Should I with faith, believing,
Insist that God make him well
    (And I *know* He can),
That nothing else will do but full recovery?

But is it best? How am I to know?
How am I to pray? I dare not ask amiss.

God knows my heart's desire, how desperately
    I want him restored to me,
    How very much I love him,
    And how I need him so.

Yes, Good knows already
So I shall abide in the comfort of His presence
And try my best to pray
    "Thy will be done"
For that prayer God can answer best.

MY HEART PONDERS . . .

Abide in me, and I in you. As the branch cannot bear fruit of itself, except it abide in the vine; no more can ye, except ye abide in me.

I am the vine, ye are the branches: He that abideth in me, and I in him, the same bringeth forth much fruit: for without me ye can do nothing.

If ye abide in me, and my words abide in you, ye shall ask what ye will, and it shall be done unto you. JOHN 15:4,5,7

And he (Christ) went forward a little, and fell on the ground, and prayed that, if it were possible, the hour might pass from him.

And he said, Abba, Father, all things are possible unto thee; take away this cup from me: nevertheless not what I will, but what thou wilt.
MARK 14:35,36

Tongue Tied

I have a speech impediment
When it comes to prayer.
Somehow my tongue is tied and words I utter
Don't sound at all as I would like them to.

Surely God must smile when I attempt
To speak His praise majestically
And get all bogged down.

Maybe there's a special language
We both could understand
With simple words and plain
Which even I could learn to pray.

Could it be the language of the heart?

MY HEART PONDERS . . .

Let the words of my mouth, and the meditation of my heart, be acceptable in thy sight, O Lord, my strength, and my redeemer. PSALM 19:14

Though I speak with the tongues of men and of angels, and have not charity (love), I am become as sounding brass, or a tinkling cymbal. 1 COR. 13:1

But when ye pray, use not vain repetitions, as the heathen do: for they think that they shall be heard for their much speaking. MATT. 6:7

For if I pray in an unknown tongue, my spirit prayeth, but my understanding is unfruitful.

What is it then? I will pray with the spirit, and I will pray with the understanding also.
1 COR. 14:14,15a

Volcanic Soil

Sudden loss
Like molten lava
Has wiped out what I love.
Now I am desolate.

Grief has no words to pray
And yet I seek out God in prayer,
For there is hope only in Him.

In His presence
I plant my tiny mustard seed of faith
In grief's volcanic soil
And leave it in His loving care.

MY HEART PONDERS . . .

My soul trusteth in thee: yea, in the shadow of thy wings will I make my refuge, until these calamities be overpast. PSALM 57:1b

Cast thy burden upon the Lord, and he shall sustain thee. PSALM 55:22a

Casting all your care upon him; for he careth for you. I PETER 5:7

He healeth the broken in heart, and bindeth up their wounds. PSALM 147:3

He that dwelleth in the secret place of the most High shall abide under the shadow of the Almighty.
PSALM 91:1

For thou art my hope, O Lord God. PSALM 71:5a

The Spirit Intercedes

I cannot always pray soul-satisfying prayers
In which quite fluently I express
My inmost lodgings and my needs and wait
    and find God's will and way.

There are times when words don't come at all
Or if I try to utter them it's like shouting
    against the wind.

I find comfort then
While quietly I wait
Remembering God's Holy Spirit maketh
    intercession for me
(And has been all along!)
In ways too marvelous to comprehend.

MY HEART PONDERS . . .

Likewise the Spirit also helpeth our infirmities: for we know not what we should pray for as we ought: but the Spirit itself maketh intercession for us with groanings which cannot be uttered.

And he that searcheth the hearts knoweth what is the mind of the Spirit, because he maketh intercession for the saints according to the will of God.

And we know that all things work together for good to them that love God, to them who are the called according to his purpose. ROMANS 8:26-28

And I will pray the Father, and he shall give you another Comforter, that he may abide with you for ever;

But the Comforter, which is the Holy Ghost, whom the Father will send in my name, he shall teach you all things, and bring all things to your remembrance, whatsoever I have said unto you.
JOHN 14:16,26